Truth and Rumors
U.S. Presidents

by Sean Stewart Price   illustrations by Eldon Doty

Consultant:
Phil Schoenberg, PhD
Professor, American History
and Government
Vaughn College of Aeronautics
and Technology
Flushing, New York

CAPSTONE PRESS
a capstone imprint

Edge Books are published by Capstone Press,
151 Good Counsel Drive, P.O. Box 669, Mankato, Minnesota 56002.
www.capstonepress.com

Printed in the United States of America in Stevens Point, Wisconsin.
092009
005619WZS10

Books published by Capstone Press are manufactured with paper
containing at least 10 percent post-consumer waste.

Library of Congress Cataloging-in-Publication Data
Price, Sean.
   U.S. presidents : truth and rumors / by Sean Stewart Price ; illustrated by Eldon Doty.
   p. cm. — (Edge books. Truth and rumors)
   Summary: "Labels common stories about former U.S. presidents as fact or fiction
and teaches readers how to tell the difference between truth and rumors" — Provided
by publisher.
   Includes bibliographical references and index.
   ISBN 978-1-4296-3952-1 (library binding)
   1. Presidents — United States — History — Miscellanea — Juvenile literature.
2. Presidents — United States — Biography — Miscellanea — Juvenile literature. 3. United
States — Politics and government — Miscellanea — Juvenile literature. I. Doty, Eldon, ill.
II. Title. III. Series.
E176.1.P973 2010
973.09'9 — dc22   **JUL 3 0 2010**   2009028651

Editorial Credits
Abby Czeskleba, editor; Tracy Davies; designer; Wanda Winch, media researcher;
   Nathan Gassman, art director; Laura Manthe, production specialist; Eldon Doty, illustrator

Photo Credits
Abraham Lincoln, Draft of the Gettysburg Address: Nicolay Copy, November 1863; Series 3, General
Correspondence, 1837–1897; The Abraham Lincoln Papers at the Library of Congress, Manuscript Division
(Washington, D. C.: American Memory Project, [2000–02]) 17 (top); Capstone Studio: Karon Dubke 29; Chippewa
Nature Center, Midland, Michigan/Oxbow Archaeologists/Scott Beld 15 (top); CORBIS: Bettmann 23 (bottom);
Courtesy Gerald R. Ford Library 24 (top), 25 (top); Courtesy Jimmy Carter Library 27 (top); The Daily Californian,
UC Berkeley 27 (bottom); iStockphoto: Bill Noll cover (red texture); John F. Kennedy Presidential Library and
Museum, Boston/Cecil Stoughton 22 (top); Library of Congress: cover (Washington, T. Roosevelt, Jackson) 4
(top), 6 (top), 7 (top), 10 (top), 12 (top), 14 (top), 16 (top), 20 (top), 26 (top); National Parks Service/ Theodore
Roosevelt Birthplace 21 (bottom); Shutterstock: Adam Radosavljevic back cover (frame), Albachiara (quill pen/inkwell,
throughout), Ali Mazraie Shadi (halftone, throughout), Anton Gvozdikov 21 (top), CLM 9 (middle), Denise Kappa
18 (bottom), hektor2 cover (gold round frames), Konrad Bak, cover, back cover (wall), RLHambley 13 (top), S.
Borisov 8 (bottom), Tara Flake 18 (top), VikaSuh (gavel, throughout); Wikipedia: KitemanSA 19 (bottom)

Table of Contents

Fact and Fiction in the White House

Quick – decide which of these stories is true:

1. Ulysses S. Grant got a $20 fine for speeding in a horse and buggy. He was the first president to get a speeding ticket while in office.

2. John F. Kennedy liked to race his red Corvette around Washington, D.C. Very few people knew about it at the time. The police kept his many speeding tickets a secret until after his death in 1963.

It's hard to tell which story is true, isn't it? Both stories seem just odd enough to be possible. We often forget that presidents can have strange habits and colorful personalities like everybody else.

Because so many people talk about U.S. presidents, it's easy to spread untrue stories. Rumors can come from any number of sources: an angry enemy, a news story with incorrect facts, even a simple misunderstanding. All of these stories can make it hard to sort out fact from **fiction**.

This book addresses some common stories about U.S. presidents. It also explains some weird-but-true tales about them. These stories show that presidents are just like the rest of us.

fiction – a story about characters or events that are not real

Answers:
1. True; 2. False

Did George Washington have wooden chompers?

What's the story?

George Washington had false teeth made of wood. These wooden teeth didn't fit well in his mouth. They made the father of our country look like he had a mouthful of mush.

1st President 1789-1797

NOT SO FAST...

Washington started losing his teeth in his 20s. Losing his teeth at such a young age forced him to wear several sets of false teeth over time. Dr. John Greenwood made one of Washington's best-known sets of dentures. The teeth in Greenwood's dentures included hippo ivory, a cow's tooth, and one of Washington's own teeth. Washington's other dentures were made of ivory.

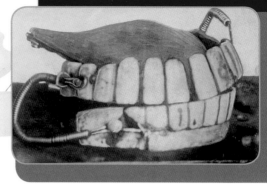

No. Washington had false teeth, but none of them were made of wood. And wow, did those false teeth hurt! Dr. Greenwood's dentures were held together by bulky metal plates and springs. Washington must have felt like he was using a machine to chew. No wonder he looks so uncomfortable in some of his portraits.

> **FACT:** Washington paid between $15 and $20 for his dentures. In the 1790s, everyday workers made about $15 a month. Only rich people could afford dentures.

The Cherry Tree — EXPOSED!

Young George Washington was a very naughty boy. As the story goes, young George chopped down his father's cherry tree when he was about 6 years old. But at least George was honest about it. Legend explains that when his dad asked, George replied, "I cannot tell a lie."

This myth has been exposed! A man named Parson Mason Weems was one of Washington's first biographers. Weems knew little about Washington's childhood. So he made up stories, like the cherry tree whopper. All of them made Washington look heroic or noble.

Did Washington throw his money around?

What's the story?

George Washington was a great athlete during his younger days. To show how strong he was, Washington threw a silver dollar across the Potomac River.

NOT SO FAST...

Washington was known for his strength. But was he really strong enough to throw a silver dollar across the Potomac? The river is more than 1 mile (1.6 kilometers) wide at places. He would've had quite the throwing arm.

No. No human, not even an athlete like Washington, could throw a silver dollar that far. Also, U.S. silver dollars were not made until 1794. By then, the 62-year-old Washington probably didn't have much of a throwing arm.

A story told by Washington's step-grandson, George Washington Parke Custis, may explain this myth. Custis claimed that Washington threw a piece of slate across the Rappahannock River near Fredericksburg, Virginia. The slate was about the size of a silver dollar. Washington threw the piece of slate 250 feet (76 meters). That's about the same length as seven school buses parked end to end.

Did John Quincy Adams give an interview while naked?

What's the story?

President John Quincy Adams gave a press interview while swimming naked in the Potomac River.

6th President   1825–1829

CONSIDER THIS...

Adams liked to skinny-dip. He snuck down to the Potomac River in Washington, D.C., early each morning when few people were around. **Journalist** Anne Royall asked Adams for interviews several times, but he refused. The story goes that Royall approached him while he was swimming one morning. She supposedly sat on his clothes until he agreed to speak with her.

Maybe. If this story is true, it probably marked the first time that a president ever gave an interview to a female reporter. In Adams' time, few women worked outside the home. Because Adams and Royall never spoke of this story, no one's sure if it really happened.

> **journalist** – someone who collects information and writes articles for newspapers, magazines, TV, or radio

Presidential Skinny-Dipping

John Quincy Adams did have other mishaps while skinny-dipping. Once, he and a servant tried to swim across the Potomac, but Adams later became exhausted by the swim. When the servant lost his clothes in the river's strong current, Adams gave the servant his own clothes. The servant then went for a carriage. Meanwhile, a naked Adams waited on the riverbank for his servant. The president never tried to swim across the Potomac again.

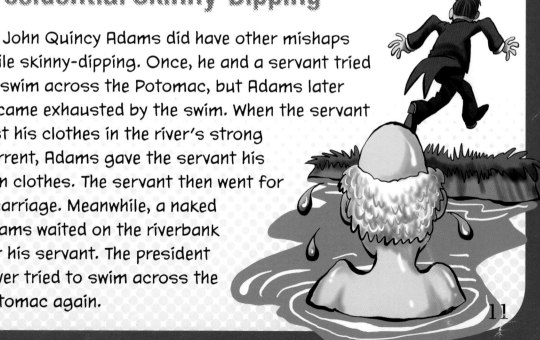

Was Andrew Jackson's parrot potty-mouthed?

7th President 1829-1837

What's the story?

President Andrew Jackson owned a parrot named Poll. Poll spoke curse words that she picked up from listening to Jackson. At Jackson's funeral, the bird flew to the dome on top of his tomb and let loose a string of cuss words.

THE EVIDENCE

Jackson was known for cussing. But cussing then was not quite the same as it is today. For instance, one of Jackson's favorite curses was "By the eternal!" A phrase like that gets yawns today, but it was somewhat shocking for the 1800s. However, Jackson also used swear words that would be familiar to our ears.

Yes. Jackson did in fact have an African grey parrot named Poll. And she picked up some of his more off-color phrases. According to witnesses, Poll interrupted Jackson's funeral by cussing. She had to be removed.

FACT: Chester A. Arthur and Franklin Pierce were the only two presidents who did not have pets in the White House.

Presidential Pets

Presidents have kept some pretty strange animals in the White House. Both John Quincy Adams and Herbert Hoover had pet alligators. Benjamin Harrison let a pair of pet opossums run around. Theodore Roosevelt had a small zoo that included a bear and a badger. But Calvin Coolidge took the prize for building a zoolike collection of animals. His pets included a pygmy hippo, a bobcat, two lion cubs, an antelope, and a wallaby.

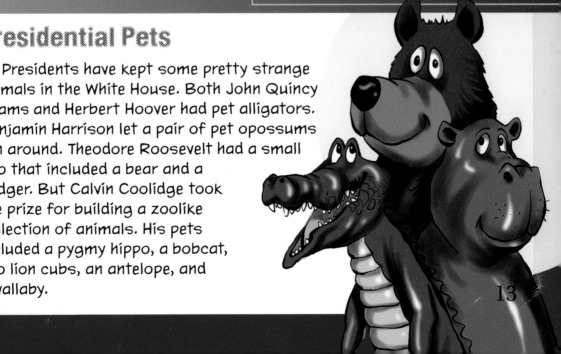

13

Did Martin Van Buren give us "OK"?

What's the story?

Martin Van Buren's nickname "Old Kinderhook" gave us the expression "OK."

8th President 1837–1841

CONSIDER THIS . . .

In the 1830s, people came up with acronyms for common sayings. It's the same thing as using BTW for "by the way" in e-mails today. But back then, people came up with acronyms like "GTDHD" for "give the devil his due." Another was "OK" for "oll korrect," a funny misspelling of "all correct." But the saying was not widely used.

GTDHD!

People running Van Buren's 1840 re-election campaign wanted something catchy to get voters' attention. The 59-year-old Van Buren was from Kinderhook, New York. He was sometimes nicknamed "Old Kinderhook." Van Buren's supporters decided to make the connection between "oll korrect" and "Old Kinderhook." His campaign workers started forming "OK" clubs and going to "OK" balls.

The VERDICT

Yes. Without Van Buren's re-election campaign, OK would never have become a popular expression. Soon people were using it to mean "all right" or "fine."

Did Abraham Lincoln write the Gettysburg Address in a rush?

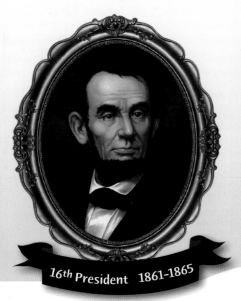

16th President 1861–1865

What's the story?

Abraham Lincoln wrote the Gettysburg Address on an envelope during his train ride to Gettysburg, Pennsylvania.

BUT CONSIDER THIS . . .

This story got started about a year after Lincoln's 1865 **assassination**. It has been repeated in history books and novels ever since. Lincoln worked long and hard on his speeches. Each one had several drafts. He would not have put off writing the Gettysburg Address until he was on the train ride to Gettysburg. Also, the trains at the time rocked and swayed. It was hard to do much writing while traveling on a train.

The VERDICT

No. Lincoln put a lot of time and effort into the Gettysburg Address. The five original copies of the speech are proof of his hard work.

Executive Mansion,
Washington, . 186

Four score and seven years ago our fathers brought forth, upon this continent, a new nation, conceived in liberty, and dedicated to the proposition that "all men are created equal."

Now we are engaged in a great civil war, testing whether that nation, or any nation so conceived, and so dedicated, can long endure. We are met on a great battle field of that war. We have come to dedicate a portion of it, as a final resting place for those who died here that the nation might live. This we may, in all propriety do. But, in a larger sense, we can not dedicate—we can not consecrate—we can not hallow, this ground— The brave men, living and dead, who struggled here, have hallowed it, far above our poor power to add or detract. The world will little note, nor long remember what we say here; while it can never forget what they did here.

It is rather for us, the living, to stand here,

assassination — the murder of a well-known or important person, such as a president

How he became Honest Abe

After Lincoln died in 1865, people who knew him began telling stories. One of those stories focused on Abe's youth in the tiny village of New Salem, Illinois. Abe was a clerk in a small store at the time. A customer named Clarissa Hornbuckle accidentally overpaid by nearly seven cents. According to the story, Abe walked 3 miles (4.8 kilometers) to pay Clarissa back. Clarissa told many people this story before she died in 1927. We know from this story and others that Lincoln's reputation for honesty was no myth.

Is Lincoln buried under the Lincoln Memorial?

What's the story?

Some people think Abraham Lincoln's body is buried under the Lincoln **Memorial**.

THE EVIDENCE

Millions of people visit the memorial each year in Washington, D.C. It makes sense that such an important figure in U.S. history would be buried in the nation's capital. The stairs are made of granite and marble, which are common tombstone materials. What's more, the memorial kind of looks like a big tomb.

No. The Lincoln Memorial was not started until 1914, long after Lincoln died. People visit the memorial to remember Lincoln, but he is actually buried in his hometown of Springfield, Illinois.

> **memorial** – something that is built or done to help people remember a person or an event

Lincoln Memorial Myths — EXPOSED!

People believe some crazy things about the Lincoln Memorial. Here are the facts behind the strangest rumors about the memorial:

The Myth: The face of General Robert E. Lee is carved in the back of Lincoln's head. General Lee led the Confederate forces during the Civil War (1861–1865).

The Truth: Sculptor Daniel Chester French intended to show Lincoln's wavy hair, nothing more. However, many visitors say they can see a face from certain angles.

The Myth: The hands on the Lincoln statue form the American Sign Language symbols for his initials.

The Truth: The sculptor simply wanted the hands to look relaxed.

The Myth: The memorial's 57 steps stand for the years of Lincoln's life.

The Truth: Lincoln was 56 years old when he died.

Did Teddy Roosevelt give us teddy bears?

What's the story?

President Theodore "Teddy" Roosevelt spared the life of a bear while hunting. This act of mercy led a toy maker to produce the first teddy bears.

26th President 1901-1909

THE EVIDENCE

In 1902, Roosevelt was on a hunting trip in Mississippi with friends. Some of the men caught a bear and tied it to a tree. They wanted to give the president the honor of killing it. But Roosevelt looked at the frightened animal and refused to shoot it.

The VERDICT

Yes. News of Roosevelt's mercy caused a toy maker to create stuffed animals named after the president. But there is an overlooked part of this story. While Roosevelt refused to kill the bear, he did let someone else shoot it.

Bulletproof Teddy

While Roosevelt was campaigning in 1912, a man shot him in the chest. The bullet should have killed Roosevelt. But a 50-page speech in his breast pocket slowed down the bullet. The wound was not serious. Yet Roosevelt was still injured and bleeding. Even so, he insisted on giving his speech before going to a hospital. Teddy was no "teddy bear."

21

Did John F. Kennedy have a secret marriage?

What's the story?

John F. Kennedy (JFK) had a secret marriage before his wedding to Jacqueline Bouvier in 1953.

35th President   1961–1963

WAIT A SECOND . . .

In 1961, rumors spread that President Kennedy had secretly married a woman back in 1947. If true, the story would ruin Kennedy politically. It would also end his marriage to wife Jacqueline. President Kennedy strongly denied the rumors. Most people believed that it was simply a political attack.

But years later, one of Kennedy's friends, Charles Spalding, claimed the story was true. Spalding said that Kennedy's father kept the matter quiet. Spalding said he and an attorney destroyed the marriage records.

The VERDICT

Probably not. Aside from Spalding's word, there is little evidence that any previous wedding took place. Durie Malcolm, the woman rumored to be JFK's first wife, died in 2008. She and Kennedy both denied they were ever married.

Was Gerald Ford a fashion model?

What's the story?

Gerald Ford worked part-time as a fashion model while he was in law school.

CONSIDER THIS . . .

During the 1930s, Gerald Ford attended Yale Law School in New Haven, Connecticut. Ford was a handsome young man. At the time, he was dating a woman named Phyllis Brown. She became a popular fashion model. Brown appeared on several magazine covers and convinced Ford to try out modeling as well.

The VERDICT

Yes. Many people believe Ford even appeared on the cover of *Cosmopolitan* with Brown. But he wasn't credited in the photo. Ford also married a former fashion model, Betty Bloomer.

Ford the klutz — EXPOSED!

President Ford tripped during a couple of public appearances in the 1970s. Comedians, especially on the TV show *Saturday Night Live (SNL)*, jumped on these missteps. SNL actors began doing imitations of Ford in which they fell all over the place. These impressions made people believe Ford was clumsy. Ironically, Ford is one of our most athletic and least clumsy former presidents. In college, he was a football player and a boxer. Even as president, Ford liked to swim and golf.

25

Was Jimmy Carter attacked by a rabbit?

What's the story?

An angry-looking rabbit tried to board Jimmy Carter's fishing boat and attack him.

39th President 1977-1981

THE EVIDENCE

Carter loved to go fishing. In 1978, a rabbit swam up to Carter's canoe while he was fishing. That was strange enough. But Carter said that the rabbit was hissing, flashing its teeth, and flaring its nostrils. Even more alarming, the rabbit tried to board Carter's boat several times. Carter swatted the rabbit away with his paddle and the rabbit swam on.

Yes. But many of Carter's own friends refused to believe the story. Fortunately the White House photographer took pictures that showed Carter was telling the truth. Nobody knows what was wrong with the rabbit.

The bunny that brought down a president

The press went wild over Carter's rabbit story. Carter's popularity was already sinking at the time. Many Americans felt that he was not providing strong leadership. News that he had been attacked by a bunny seemed like the last straw. Newspapers and comedians told countless jokes. The rabbit story made Carter look foolish. He lost the 1980 election against Ronald Reagan.

FACT OR FICTION?:
How to Tell the Difference

There are many funny and off-beat stories about U.S. presidents. In the following stories, see if you can tell which ones are real and which ones are made up.

1. An 11-year-old girl's letter gave Abraham Lincoln the idea for growing his beard.

2. The Baby Ruth candy bar is named after Grover Cleveland's daughter Ruth. As an infant, she was known as "Baby Ruth."

3. William Howard Taft was so big that he often got stuck in the White House bathtub. He replaced the tub with one big enough to seat four normal-sized men.

Which of these stories is true? Believe it or not, they're all true. Yet they don't tell you the whole story.

Take Baby Ruth, for example. The candy bar was officially named after Ruth Cleveland. But it was not introduced until 1921. That was 24 years after Grover

Cleveland left office and 17 years after Ruth had died. But 1921 was around the time that baseball great Babe Ruth rose to fame. The candy company didn't want to pay Babe Ruth for using his name. So the company named the candy bar after "Baby Ruth" Cleveland instead.

To sort out the truth from the rumors, do research to get the whole story. Use the Internet to look up experts at museums, history centers, and universities. Call these places and ask questions. It is also good to use books and well-known newspapers. Sometimes it's hard to tell if a source is reliable or not. When in doubt, ask a librarian. Do your research, and you'll have no problem telling rumors from the truth.

Glossary

assassination (uh-sass-uh-NAY-shuhn) — the murder of a well-known or important person, such as a president

biography (bye-OG-ruh-fee) — a book that tells someone's life story

dentures (DEN-churz) — a set of false teeth

fiction (FIK-shuhn) — a story about characters or events that are not real

ivory (EYE-vur-ee) — the natural substance from which the tusks and teeth of some animals are made

journalist (JUR-nuhl-ist) — someone who collects information and writes articles for newspapers, magazines, TV, or radio

memorial (muh-MOR-ee-uhl) — something that is built or done to help people remember a person or an event

nickname (NIK-name) — a familiar or shortened form of a name

reputation (rep-yuh-TAY-shuhn) — one's character, as judged by other people

Read More

Britton, Tamara L. *Theodore Roosevelt.* The United States Presidents. Edina, Minn.: ABDO, 2009.

Gaines, Ann. *George Washington: Our First President.* Presidents of the U.S.A. Mankato, Minn.: Child's World, 2009.

Rappaport, Doreen. *Abe's Honest Words: The Life of Abraham Lincoln.* New York: Hyperion Books for Children, 2008.

Internet Sites

FactHound offers a safe, fun way to find Internet sites related to this book. All of the sites on FactHound have been researched by our staff.

Here's all you do:

Visit *www.facthound.com*

FactHound will fetch the best sites for you!

Index